NICOLÒ BOLLA

Your Move to Italy

Learn How to Move and to Settle with Comfort in Italy

NICOLÒ BOLLA
Head of accounting Bolla

TABLE OF CONTENTS

INTRODUCTION

With a whopping 55 World Heritage sites, Italy is a major global tourism destination.

Whether you like art, seaside, immaculate mountains or charming countryside, Italy has everything you are looking for in a destination.

It is a common feeling for non-Italians to find great ways to do business and make money easily in Italy. It is a big country, with a strong economy, and multiple opportunities. After a good brainstorming session with your friends or fellow expats, you have finally found the next big thing in Italy, and you are 100% sure that you will make money off it in a couple of years.

Not too fast!

Your business plan did not account for two typical Italian features: high taxes and byzantine bureaucracy.

Then, you start wandering around different online groups and blogs and hear horrific stories about businesses which were choked by the horrendous greediness of the tax office as well as the overall lack of business acumen of the Italian public offices in general.

Those who made it have to face daily challenges and crawl through a complex, harsh, and unfriendly environment.

Despite author's different take on the Italian business environment, this picture is far from being inaccurate as Italy tops the list of the countries with the highest taxation. This is discouraging, to say the least, if you want to start a business!

If you are asking yourself: How can I move to Italy? I am sure you will find a practical and suitable answer to your question.

There are multiple ways to deal through the system and prosper in this business environment, and Nicolò Bolla can guide you through the whole process of planning your tax expenditure wisely.

In this book, Nicolò Bolla will provide real life examples and case stories developed through his experience to help you understand how to make the most out of your income in a legal, honest, and safe way.

AUTHOR

Nicolò Bolla is an international tax accountant (chartered in Italy and the UK) with a wide expertise on personal and business taxation issues across jurisdiction. He is also a trusted immigration attorney.

With a strong education background acquired in Italy and the USA, he proficiently helped thousands of foreigners to develop a tax and immigration strategy to move to Italy, efficiently exploiting the best strategies and tax breaks available.

Through seminars across Italy, Europe, and the US, he is empowering individuals to develop their best immigration strategy, combining it with the most advanced tax strategies available in Italy.

facebook.com/accountingbolla

linkedin.com/in/accountingbolla/

instagram.com/accountingbolla

www.accountingbolla.com

n.bolla@accountingbolla.com

1

WHY MOVE TO ITALY

Who wouldn't want to live in Italy, Europe's most intriguing and seductive country? Think about its warmth, style, and wonderful food; its people, the ancient cultures, the landscapes; its art treasures, its immaculate countryside, and its busy cities. Italy is a gem with a magnificent past and a bright future ahead.

You're not limited to the major cities; Italy's landscapes are as gorgeous as they are diverse: historic walled towns, timeless villages, and fields covered with yellow sunflowers.

Italy also provides great job opportunities and a thriving economy, especially in certain areas in the North. Italy is becoming more international and more diverse, and it is attracting foreign investors to invest in its economy.

Italy is also a founding member of the EU, and it is a dream to millions of people overseas.

Whether you are looking for job opportunities, a better lifestyle, or investing, Italy is the right place for you.

1.1. RETIRE UNDER THE ITALIAN SUN

Let's be honest, who wouldn't want to retire in Italy?

Italians are among the longest living people on Earth, whether it is the food, the climate, the living standards, or the healthcare system.

From 2019 on you have another reason to retire in Italy: a tax regime tailored to pensioners.

If you are an individual who:
- Receives a non-Italian pension treatment;
- Has not been a tax resident of Italy in the previous 5 years;

- Moves into a qualifying municipality (a municipality with 20,000 inhabitants or less located in the South).

You can benefit of a flat 7% tax on EVERY foreign sourced income for 5 years, and there is no wealth tax to be paid!

This means that if you qualify you can abide to every tax obligation by just paying a 7% tax.

Imagine that you realize capital gains or earn interests and dividends from your investment portfolio; you only pay 7% on that.

Also, if you want to cash out your whole pension funds, you can do it paying this 7% tax and that is it; you can now dispose of your monies freely.

Anyway, there is a downside on that. Since the 7% flat tax is a substitute tax, you cannot claim any deductible items against it, but more importantly you cannot offset any withholding tax paid abroad.

1.2. ECONOMIC BENEFITS

1.2.1. ITALIAN TAX SYSTEM

The Italian income tax system is called IRPEF, and it is based on progressive brackets, meaning that the more money you earn, the more you pay as brackets go up from 23% up to 43%.

However, the Italian tax system is based on the concept of the capacità contributiva which can be easily translated as the ability to pay, and this is not based exclusively on the income available to an individual but on other matters as well.

Let's think about two taxpayers: for simplicity we will call them Antonio and Battista. Antonio is a single adult male who is employed and makes around 50k of gross income per year; Battista makes the same amount of money, but he is married, his wife is not employed, and they have two young kids to take care of. Would you think that they both have same ability to contribute? Of course, not!

The legislator has, therefore, thought about that and introduced multiple tax-deductible items which are divided into two categories:

1. Tax deductible Items against income;

2. Tax deductible Items against gross tax.

The first ones reduce your taxable income; therefore, the tax savings is equal to the marginal tax rate paid. In this category we find:
- Mandatory Social Security Contribution (INPS);
- Voluntary Social Security Contribution (INPS);
- Voluntary Private Pensions Contribution;
- Spouse alimony;
- Donations to NGO and non-profit organizations.

As an example, assuming you are a top rate taxpayer and you decide to contribute € 2,000.00 towards your voluntary private pension fund, you will then save € 860.00 on your tax bill claiming a refund (€ 2.000,00 * 43%). If your marginal tax rate is 23%, your tax saving is reduced to € 560.00.

The items falling in the second category reduce your gross tax. In this case the deductible expenditure is multiplied by a coefficient set by the law (19%-36%-50%-65%-75%-85%). In this category we have, among others:
- Health expenses;
- Vet expenses;
- School expenses;
- Family dependents;
- Main residency loan interests paid;

- House renovation expenses;
- Energy efficiency house improvements;
- Furniture purchase expense;
- Lease paid.

A € 1,000.00 medical bill generates a tax saving of € 190.00 since the coefficient is 19%. Your total deductible items cannot exceed your gross tax; in other words, the minimum amount of tax payable is 0. You cannot have a negative amount of taxes payable, and you cannot carry forward (or backward) any unclaimed tax-deductible item.

Now you can easily understand that despite a high gross tax payable the tax expenditure might be little to none. If you want to compare tax systems, you must do it evaluating the NET tax paid.

Because of that the Italian tax system ranks very competitive among the developed countries, surprising many who think otherwise.

Throughout the years, the Italian legislator introduced various new taxes that replaced IRPEF. They are called imposta sostitutiva (substitute tax.) As the word says, substitute tax rates replace one or more taxes; think about the cedolare secca, regime forfettario, capital gains tax etc. They all replace IRPEF, regional and municipal surcharges, in some other cases registrar tax, VAT, as well as stamp duty. In some cases, you can opt between IRPEF tax and the substitute tax (think about IRPEF vs. cedolare secca) whereas in other circumstances you are obligated to adopt the substitute tax over IRPEF (capital gains is the best example).

Normally, substitute taxes have lower rates and are flat, and they appear far more advantageous than the regular taxes. Sometimes, it is not the case, and I will explain you why. Substitute taxes do not allow you to claim any deductible items against them; therefore, your gross tax is always equal to your net tax. Any tax-deductible item is then wasted.

Despite this, substitute taxes make it easier to plan how much your expenditure will look like; you do not have to perform complex calculations; however, you might end up losing money as you will not be able to claim your deductions.

The bottom line is simple: taxes are cash outflows, and you must never compare the tax rates payable - you must always compare the tax rates paid! I don't think you care much if your gross tax rate is 23% or 43%: you care about how many Euros fall out of your pocket when paying taxes. Am I right?

Furthermore, there is no one fits all solution; taxes are a personal matter, and they are affected by your personal situation; thus, any tax minimization strategy must be carefully tailored to your specific needs.

Please, do not rely on a Friend of a friend of advice, or DIY. You can hurt yourself badly and the advice of an experienced accountant is always worth.

The Italian sales tax system is based on IVA, having three main brackets: 4% for essential products and primary residence, 10% on food and beverages, and 22% rate on any other product service.

Real estate is taxed at purchase and possession. If you buy a property, you are expected to pay between 2% and 9% on registrar tax, while you pay roughly 1% tax on your real estate on ownership.

If you are a resident for tax purposes in Italy, you must also disclose your foreign held assets (bank account, real estate, cryptocurrencies, investment portfolio etc.) and pay wealth tax at a 0.2% rate.

Having said so, Italy provides for countless tax breaks helping to reduce your tax burden. For instance, you can get 50% tax back on every Innovative Startup investment, or up to 110% for any qualifying home improvement.

The efficient use of tax breaks is fundamental to master the Italian tax system and to enjoy your Dolce Vita without any adverse tax consequence.

1.2.2. WHAT TO KNOW ABOUT TAXES: HOW DO TAXES IMPACT YOUR BUSINESS?

The main priority of every business should be operating in compliance with the laws and the applicable regulations, the second priority is to become efficient regards to taxes and social security.

At the end of the day taxes are a cash outflow to your business and minimizing it or being efficient is crucial and it can affect greatly the returns as of your business plan. It would not be nice to realize that all your efforts are wiped out because of taxes.

Professional businesses have more options to choose regards to taxation, whilst non-professional ones are bound to a specific tax regime.

The Italian tax system is one of the most articulated and byzantine tax systems in the Western world. Italy is known for its strong bureaucracy and unfriendly tax system.

We have to say that the Italian tax system is very complicated, but from its complications, you can find great opportunities and loopholes to minimize the tax burden. Don't be fooled by the high nominal tax rates! If you use your tax deductions and breaks efficiently, you can greatly reduce your taxation to minimal and affordable levels.

Let's have a look into the overall income tax system in Italy.

1.2.3. 5% INCOME TAX. HOW CAN YOU BEAT THAT?

This would be headline of my advertising online: the display would be a really sad family that looks at their tax return and after my advice they are able to enjoy their extra money, because they just paid 5% tax!

Honestly, how can you get any lower than 5%?

The ad would also include a tiny asterisk saying Terms and Conditions Apply, and here we go…

Let's call things by their name: the 5% tax is called Regime For-fettario, and it is a tax regime introduced in 2014 and boosted during 2018 to include more taxpayers into this advantageous regime.

First of all, only individuals can access it and there are multiple constraints:

– You cannot make more than € 65,000.00 in revenue;
– You cannot have other sources of income exceeding € 65,000.00;
– You cannot have a controlling interest in any company or partnership (either directly or indirectly);
– Your sources of income must be located within the EU for at least 75%;
– You cannot entertain business with your previous employer within 2 years of your dismissal.

Scrolling through the conditions, it is clear that not everyone can access this regime straightaway. Furthermore, the 5% tax only lasts for the first 5 years of a new trade; from the 6th year on the tax rate is increased to 15%.

Let me explain how the tax calculation works. Every Partita IVA has an activity code and based on that the tax authorities have determined a coefficient of profitability which can range from 40% to 78% of the revenue.

Assuming you are a business consultant whose revenue is € 50,000.00 per year, your coefficient is 78%; therefore, your taxable income under this regime is € 39,000.00.

It doesn't matter how many costs related to your activity you have to pay, you cannot write them off for tax purpose; in the end it is called forfettario because it forfeits how to pay taxes.

In our scenario you will pay € 1,950.00 of taxes and € 10,000.00 in INPS payments. Is this the best deal?

Also remember that as a substitute tax you cannot deduct any item against income or taxes; therefore, you cannot claim any family dependents, health expenses, house renovation costs, as well as any other deductible items.

You will pay both taxes with no further reductions; moreover, after 5 years your tax payment increases to € 5,850.00

Once again, is this still a great deal?

Highlighting the main advantages of this regime:

- You do not charge VAT, which becomes handy when you deal with final clients;
- You do not suffer any withholding tax;
- Accounting is simplified;
- Your tax accountant will charge you less;
- You can still hire people without paying any IRAP;
- No E-invoices.

This regime is fantastic if you already have other sources of income up to € 65,000.00 (employment, rental income etc.); therefore, any extra activity will normally carry a higher tax rate, and you can actually invoice another € 65,000.00 at 5%. Potentially you can have € 130,000.00 in revenues and half of it is taxable at 5%!

It is also great if you do not bear any (or limited) cost for your business, such as a business consultant or an online marketer; in this case you are given a 22% ex-gratia taxable income reduction.

Finally, if you are an artisan or a trader, you can benefit a 35% reduction of your INPS payments.

On the other hand, should you have to bear many more costs than 22%, this regime might be disadvantageous as accounting for them would reduce your taxable income, in turn reducing INPS payment and possibly tax payments.

The only deduction you can claim under the forfettario regime is the INPS payments, and all the remaining deductions will not be available to you. If you don't have any, no big deal; otherwise, you should also account for this loss.

Often, if you do not have high levels of income, the regime forfettario is not convenient as you will have to pay tax from the first penny you make; on the contrary, the IRPEF regime up to € 10,000.00 does not generate any tax liability.

If you trade with countries that apply withholding tax for foreign payment, you will not be able to deduct them given that you operate under the regime forfettario.

Finally, the € 65,000.00 cap can be a constraint for growth as often you are not incentivized to grow the business more as you hit the threshold.

Once again, make your math and evaluate which solution provides you with the better cash outflow!

1.2.4. TAXES ON HOUSE PURCHASE

Italy is undeniably one of the most charming countries in the world, attracting the interest of many individuals all around the globe. Italy is a destination that many people want to call home.

The Italian house market had definitely attracted the interest of investors all around the globe, so let's take a look at the taxes payable once you purchase your property in Italy.

Taxes greatly depend on the type of property and the classification of the seller, but prior to digging into them let me explain the value on which you calculate taxes, called *valore catastale*.

The formula is the following:

$$\textit{Rendita catastale} \times 1.05 \times 1.20$$

Let's say that the rendita catastale of your property is € 511.29, and the value on which you calculate property taxes is € 64,422.54 regardless of the price you pay for the property itself.

Residential property

If you purchase residential property from a private individual or from a company that does not charge Value Added Tax (VAT), the following taxes are payable:

TAX	AMOUNT
IMPOSTA DI REGISTRO	9% of the cadastral value
IMPOSTA IPOTECARIA	€ 50,00
IMPOSTA CATASTALE	€ 50,00

If the seller is a company charging VAT, the following taxes are payable:

TAX	AMOUNT
IVA	10% of the property value (22% if the property belongs to A/01-A/08-A/09)
IMPOSTA DI REGISTRO	€ 200,00
IMPOSTA IPOTECARIA	€ 200,00
IMPOSTA CATASTALE	€ 200,00

It is possible to reduce taxes payable at purchase if the residential property is elected as *main residency*. In such a case, taxes are as follows:

TAX	AMOUNT
IMPOSTA DI REGISTRO	2% of the cadastral value
IMPOSTA IPOTECARIA	€ 50,00
IMPOSTA CATASTALE	€ 50,00

If the seller is a company charging VAT, the following taxes are payable:

TAX	AMOUNT
IVA	4% of the property value
IMPOSTA DI REGISTRO	€ 200,00
IMPOSTA IPOTECARIA	€ 200,00
IMPOSTA CATASTALE	€ 200,00

To benefit from the main residency tax reduction, the buyer is required to move his/her residency to the **same municipality** in which the property is located within *18* months of the date on the purchase deed.

As a buyer, you are not required to move to the property you purchased, for the simple fact that your property might require renovations that take longer than *18* months.

Failure to move your residency within *18* months of the purchase deed will make you liable to pay the difference between the taxes paid and the taxes payable on top of a fine amounting to 30% of any tax due.

Rushing to apply for residency in Italy is a top mistake made by expats: you must bear in mind that if you are registered as a resident in Italy for the most part of the year, you ARE A TAX RESIDENT!

This means that you must file your taxes and disclose your foreign held assets. Since you have 18 months to do that, you can choose the right time to move, as well as restructure your wealth and income to minimize your tax exposure once you become resident of Italy. So many people, considering a registrar tax saving, end up with a bad deal on income taxes; don't be one of those, please.

1.2.5. CEDOLARE SECCA

If you rent a residential property or a local shop, you can opt for another type of taxation called *cedolare secca* consisting of a substitute rental tax to claim against:
- IRPEF;
- Regional and municipal surcharges;
- Registrar tax;
- Stamp duty.

Fundamentally, you do not pay any registrar tax nor stamp duty at registration and at every annual anniversary.

You will then tax your rental income at a flat 21% tax.

This seems a great deal! The minimum IPREF tax bracket is 23%, so you must pay less, right? Not too fast.

Remember that the Cedolare Secca is a substitute tax so you cannot claim any deductible items against it.

Think about the case when you have performed renovation works in your property or you have other deductions available; you might end up paying less tax with IRPEF!

Once again, what you have to do is to compare NET TAXES payable.

Normally the Cedolare Secca is very convenient if you have other sources of income as you already pay enough taxes making it convenient to exploit a flat 21% tax.

On top of it, the required annual compliance is much lower as you do not have to pay the annual registrar tax (and pay the consultant to administer your tax affairs).

1.2.6. NEW RESIDENTS TAX REGIMES

Italy recently introduced advantageous tax regimes for new residents of Italy. This is an attempt by the Italian government to make its jurisdiction more attractive to foreign individuals.

Employed and self-employed who transfer their residency to Italy enjoy 70% tax exemption on their income, meaning that whatever they earn, 70% of it is not taxed at all for 5 years. The percentage is increased to 90% if the taxpayer lives in a Southern area.

The conditions to be met are quite easy. You must:
- Become a tax resident of Italy;
- Not be a tax resident of Italy in the previous 2 (or 5 years);
- Remain in Italy for at least two tax years.
-

Assuming your income is € 50,000.00 you pay tax on only € 15,000.00, and if you relocated to the South your taxable income is further reduced to € 5,000.00. Note that unlike the regime forfettario, you have no maximum income cap and you can still claim tax deductible items against your gross tax.

If you move to Naples, you start suffering taxation on your income if you make more than € 100,000. Don't believe it? Guess how much tax you pay on € 10,000, since 90% of your income is tax free.

In 2015, Italy introduced a € 100,000 flat tax for new residents to claim against any foreign income. It doesn't matter how much money you make, you pay that flat tax against your whole income. You can also extend it to any of your family members for an extra € 25,000.

This scheme lasts up to 15 years and allows you to repatriate your monies. Unlike other regimes overseas (most notably the UK Remittance Basis Charge – RBC), the taxpayer can spend the money in Italy without any further charge.

Furthermore, no wealth tax nor Controlled Foreign Companies rule applies to the taxpayer.

Finally, Italy introduced a 7% flat tax for pensioners relocating to Southern Regions. To qualify, the taxpayer must receive a foreign pension and relocate to a qualifying municipality.

A qualifying municipality is any town with 20,000 inhabitants or less located in the Southern regions of Abruzzo, Apulia, Basilicata, Calabria, Campania, Molise, Sardinia, and Sicily.

Further qualifying municipalities are located in Lazio, Le Marche, and Umbria. However, such towns must have a population of 3,000 or less.

The 7% tax covers any foreign income for 10 years after the taxpayer moves to Italy, also avoiding the disclosure of any foreign held assets and any wealth tax payment.

If you are a new resident of Italy, you have various option to greatly reduce your tax burden for the first 10 years of residency.

1.2.7. HOUSE RENOVATION

Every house requires renovation or restoration from time to time. The Italian government has set up a series of tax incentives to facilitate house renovations, seismic structural improvements, and energy efficient investments.

The whole rationale behind this choice is to reduce the damages and risks caused by aged properties and to reduce the potential victims due to seismic events, which from time to time hit Italy in different areas.

Before explaining the different types of tax deductions, I would like to identify who can benefit of such deductions.

REMEMBER: To benefit of the tax deductions, you need to pay IRPEF in Italy!

The following categories:
- Owner;
- Usufruct holder;
- Tenant;
- Partnerships and corporations;
- Civil union partner;
- Family member of the owner.

The tax-deductible expenses refer to:
- Extraordinary maintenance;
- Energy efficiency investments;
- Restoration and renovation;
- Seismic improvements.

These expenses are tax deductible if referred to a single property or to the common areas of a condominium.

The maximum amount of tax-deductible expense is € 96.000,00 per property; the tax-deductible part is generally 50%, and it is discounted in 10 years.

Assuming you have paid € 20.000,00 to renovate your property, the total tax deduction is € 10.000,00. Since you will benefit this tax saving for the following 10 years, you will save € 1.000,00 in tax every tax year.

All you have to do is to pay the invoice using a special type of bank transfer called "bonifico ristrutturazioni", file your taxes, and then keep the proper documentation for inspection.

In the previous case, you have to make sure that you pay at least € 1,000.00 per year in tax.

Assuming your gross tax liability is € 900.00, your tax liability will drop to € 0.00, but you have no chance to recoup the € 100.00 unused tax deduction.

If the same investments would have been done into new solar panels, the tax-deductible part is raised to 65%. Considering your initial investment of € 20,000.00, you are entitled to a tax credit of € 13,000.00 to be used in ten years, hence € 1,300.00 per year.

If you spend money on seismic improvements to your property, the tax-deductible part is raised to 70% of the expenditure given that the seismic rate increases by one category. A further raise to 80% is granted if the seismic rate improves to two categories.

An extra 5% benefit is granted to condominium properties, adjusting the tax-deductible part to 75% and 85% respectively.

Contrary to the previous tax-deductible items, the seismic improvement expenses are deductible in 5 years.

Assuming an expenditure of € 80,000.00 that increases the seismic rate of one category, the tax-deductible part is € 56,000.00. In such case, you can benefit of a tax credit amounting to € 11,200.00 every year.

Given that many people cannot recoup all the taxes back (as they do not pay that much), since 2019 you can transfer your tax credit to the company performing the work, and they can offset it against their taxes.

If you cannot claim all your taxes back, it definitely makes sense to do it!

As you might understand, every time you decide to renovate your property you have to talk to your tax accountant to understand if you pay enough tax to have a substantial benefit from such renovations.

It is also possible to "pay" the individual or the company performing the work with the tax credit, transferring the right to deduct such expenses in their tax return, rather than in yours. I personally know few companies that use the technique, but this can also be a good option to optimize each other's taxes.

1.2.8. SUPERBONUS 110%

In the summer after the 2020 lockdown, Italy has introduced the Superbonus 110% scheme to boost the Italian economy, to improve the ecological transition of the economy, and to reduce the non-renewable energy dependency.

The Superbonus 110% is a temporary uplift of the aforementioned house renovation schemes. If you perform any seismic improvement to your home, you can claim the 110% uplift.

On the energy efficiency side, you must meet two conditions:
1. Replace your heating system or external thermal insulation;
2. Increase the building's overall energy efficiency of at least two categories.

If you meet the two above conditions, you can also claim the relief on other energy efficient improvements such as:
- Solar Panels;
- Batteries;
- E-vehicles charging stations;
- Double (triple) glazed windows;
- Home building automations.

The Superbonus 110% is spread out in 5 years, and it can be traded against the invoice (invoice discount) or you can pay cash and trade it to a bank to recoup the cash back.

1.2.9. FINANCIAL INCOME

Individuals who generate financial income through Italian banks and financial institutions generally do not disclose anything in their tax return, as taxes are already paid by the bank itself.

If you have any financial income (such as interests, dividends, and/or capital gains) located abroad you must disclose it in your tax return and pay the appropriate taxes (income and wealth taxes).

The general rate is a substitute tax of 26%. You need then to disclose your financial income in your tax return and self-assess the tax you owe.

Unfortunately, you cannot claim any tax paid abroad as well as any tax withheld by the foreign country bank as the substitute tax does not allow it.

It is only possible to tax interests from bank accounts or certificate of deposits at the regular IRPEF rates instead of 26% rates. In such case you can claim a foreign tax credit.

A good management of your financial position includes the search of a country that does not charge any withholding tax with Italy; normally this country is Malta. It makes sense on a tax perspective to move your assets to a country that does not levy a withholding tax as you will then only pay 26% just like every other Italian, and you will not suffer the injustice of summing up taxes in two countries.

Regarding capital gains and losses, you must know that Italy does not allow any carryback of a capital loss; any loss can be carried forward for 5 years, and after that period of time it is wasted. Because of that, if you must sell mixed assets which stand at gains and at loss, it is imperative to sell assets standing at loss first.

The major mistake that new residents do is forgetting to uplift the value of latent capital gains once they become tax resident of Italy.

Imagine that you have an investment portfolio that you build throughout your whole life; the oldest investments are standing at a great gain. Imagine also that you decide to move to Italy and then you need funds for yourself, and you decide to sell your investments.

According to the Italian tax laws the WHOLE capital gain is taxable in Italy at 26%! This means that your base value is the value of the day on which you bought the shares, not the day you moved your tax residency to Italy (like many professionals improperly confirm).

This is a really bad deal, but what can you do? Did I already talk about B&B? This is a different bed and breakfast: it is the name of a common tax strategy dealing with financial income. It only works if the country in which the asset is located has a lower tax rate compared to Italy.

This strategy is very simple; prior moving your tax residency to Italy, you sell your assets standing at gain, and you repurchase them the day after (now you got why is it called B&B?).

This allows you to reduce your tax exposure since your asset value is rebased and the gain taxable in Italy will then be greatly reduced.

1.2.10. BUSINESS SETUP

To understand how to efficiently start your business, you must be aware of the different options available in Italy. This decision is fundamental, and it reverberates every tax decision made after. Leaving on the right foot is a great advice, especially when it comes to tax decisions, but let's dig deeper.

Partita Iva

The Partita IVA is the Italian VAT number; many of you are confused by the fact that it mentions the word IVA (IVA=VAT), implying that you must charge VAT on your goods and services.

This is not the case as depending on the tax regime you might charge VAT or not; nonetheless, you cannot trade without a Partita IVA, which is required to operate as a self-employed, sole proprietor, partnership, corporation, association, and other nonprofits.

How do you get a Partita IVA and which information is required?

The process to get a Partita IVA is quite straightforward; you can do it in person at the tax office or delegate an accountant to get a Partita IVA online, and the procedure normally takes 24 hours to be completed. Once you have your Partita IVA on hand you can start trading!

To get a Partita IVA, you must supply some information, which normally is:

1. Full name;
2. Codice Fiscale;
3. Residency address;
4. Type of activity performed;
5. Bookkeeping registered address (it can be your accountant);
6. Day on which you started trading.

I would like to grab your attention on point n. 4; this is by far the most important choice and where you need to get a tailored advisory of the matter; choosing the activity performed is crucial and reverberates its consequences forward.

Not every activity can attract special tax regimes, and some activities require you to charge VAT while some others do not (thus creating a preferential cash flow for activities that do not charge output VAT).

Based on the activity code you might have different options as far as INPS regime, or you might be required to register at the Chamber of Commerce or not.

But the most important part is that different activities have different controls by the tax office, as they fall into different categories.

Despite you can change, add, or amend the activity code down the road, starting off with the right foot is definitely better.

Once again, your tax advisor can help you out greatly at this stage!

Partita Iva individuale
This is the easiest form of trade adopted by freelance, self-employed, and sole traders.

The Partita IVA can be requested online and, depending on the type of activity, a Chamber of Commerce registration might be required.

Trading under the Partita IVA is relatively simple as the accounting requirements are reduced compared to other more sophisticated structures.

The undeniable advantages of trading as a Partita IVA are:
- No notary required;
- No paid-up capital requirements;
- No board of trustees meeting as well as ordinary and extraordinary general meeting;
- No annual account filing as well as no mandatory books and registrars required;
- No wound up required once the business is ceased;
- Fewer bureaucracy involved.

This is the preferred structured adopted for early-stage trades and for individuals who are not keen to adopt more complex organization of the business. However, it is also important to highlight the main disadvantages associated with this simplified structure:
- The individual carries unlimited liability for his trade, putting the personal wealth at risk;
- The individual can be declared bankrupt;
- There is no possibility of delegating decision making (and the subsequent responsibilities);
- The individual credit score cannot be split from the business one; therefore, the trader can jeopardize the personal credit score;
- The individual pays income taxes regardless of the cash flows (often time you end up paying income taxes on income you did not even cash yet!);
- The tax office can audit your business AND personal income at the same time.

Are you still sure you want to trade as a sole proprietor?

In my experience people tend to listen to the good part (advantages) and often times forget about the bad part (disadvantages); if you want to be smart about your taxes, you must ALWAYS plan according to the worst-case scenario!

Società di persone

In other jurisdictions you refer them as Partnerships. In fact, partners are taxed on the income generated by the Società depending on the holding they have.

You need a notary to set up a Società di persone, and you require at least two partners. There are two main types of partnerships:
- Società in nome collettivo (SNC);
- Società in accomandita semplice (SAS).

In the first one EVERY partner has unlimited liability, while in the second one there must be at least on partner with unlimited liability and at least another one with limited liability.

SAS is therefore a hybrid partnership, and it is normally preferred than *SNC*; both of them require a notary to set them up but, and unlike *società di capitali* (see below), they have simplified accounting regimes and are passthrough entities.

SAS and *SNC* can also appoint managing director which does not make a difference in term of taxation the director pays; however, you can start claiming refunds and expenses which are not taxable for the director.

Being a passthrough entity means that the income is taxed on the partners based on their personal tax rates; the partnership does not pay any corporate tax, and there is no double taxation at company and individual return levels.

A *società di persone* is more preferable than a Partita Individuale for a main tax purpose. Imagine that you make around € 100,000 of taxable income; in such case you will be a higher rate taxpayer.

If a partnership does the same taxable income with two partners, both of them will have a taxable income of € 50,000 reducing the overall taxes to be paid.

The main drawback is the unlimited liability suffered by the partners, and there is no mitigation of that.

Società di capitali

A *società di capitali* is a limited company. Italy has two types of companies:
- Società a responsabilità limitata (SRL);
- Società per Azioni (SPA).

The first one is a regular limited company, while the second one is a public company.

To set up an SRL, you need at least one shareholder and a minimum paid up capital of € 1; this form of company is often time preferred due to the unlimited liability that shareholders have against any potential creditor.

You cannot risk more than the paid-up capital. That's it!

A Società di capitali has a more complex accounting. You must file the accounts annually, and profits are liable to corporate tax and income tax (once paid out).

In case of bankruptcy, unlike the other setup options, the shareholders cannot be declared bankrupt.

In my opinion, there is not a preferred business set up, a sort of one that fits all solution, yet you must well understand your current position, your future goals, and choose the best solution for your needs.

Of course, you will need a smart accountant to help you out!

1.2.11. VAT DIRECT REGISTRATION AND MOSS

Every single day we hear a headline about e-commerce; it definitely revolutionized all our lives and the pattern of consumption of EVERY person in the western world.

Economies have been integrating faster, and the competition has proved stiffer since the entry barriers to market have reduced, and logistics has become more efficient and cheaper.

In other words, e-commerce is taking over the world and this trend does not seem to be stopped anytime soon. Giant companies and global conglomerates operating in the traditional retail business have suffered greatly from the competition of online based platforms.

Considering that, the EU has introduced a new system to help businesses who perform online selling B2C, as VAT rates should be paid at the rates of the destination country, not the source one. This has been done to avoid the localization of certain businesses in countries with a more favorable VAT regime for certain products.

Different VAT rates could have easily led to a distortion in the competition within the European Union countries.

At the moment, you can sell freely online within the whole EU with your national VAT number; however, once you reach a certain threshold of business in a tax year you need to obtain a VAT number from the destination country, and you will then pay the local VAT rates.

This has to be done for EVERY country once you exceed the threshold.

Back in the days you should have either established a local branch or nominate a local fiscal representative for your foreign company; the process required a lot of bureaucracy to be passed and it took time.

Furthermore, whenever you establish a local branch, the local jurisdiction requires you to pay income tax on the income you made in that country; the VAT direct registration allows you to have a local VAT number, but you do not have to pay any income tax in the destination country as you are not established there for income tax purposes.

Assuming you have an online business in Italy, and you start selling in France and Spain; until you reach the number of sales of € 35,000.00 per country, you can still charge your home country VAT rate.

From the moment you exceed the threshold, you are required to get a local VAT number and comply with the local VAT laws, filing return and paying tax at the required deadlines.

At the moment Italy has a threshold of € 35,000.00.

In my experience, I advise to get the VAT number before reaching the threshold, as in Italy the process is totally paper based and only the central office can dispatch it. Normally it takes 2-3 months to get it, and since you do not have a VAT number you cannot legally trade in that market!

A different way of dealing with the same VAT problem is MOSS – Mini One Stop Shop. It has been created specifically for non-material products, such as software, licenses, and other online tools.

Back in the days, companies used to base their business in a country where there was no VAT charge for such products; therefore, they had no VAT to pay.

Changing the rule in favor of the VAT rate of the final client residency country required the introduction of the MOSS.

Unlike VAT direct registration, you do not need to obtain a VAT number from the local country tax office, yet you always charge your local home country VAT rate and then file a quarterly statement recapping the different sales in each EU country.

After that, you are required to pay or claim a refund on the VAT charged in each place.

1.2.12. VAT DEDUCTIBILITY

The VAT code art. 19bis1, sets out which items are not deductible for VAT purposes; there is no ground to challenge this decision as it is set by a statute law.

According to it you cannot recover VAT:
- 100% of any item which is not inherent to your business;
- 100% VAT on entertainment expenses;
- 100% VAT on residential property purchase;
- 60% of VAT paid on any road vehicle purchase;
- 60% of VAT paid for gas related to vehicles;

- 50% VAT paid on mixed used items;
- 50% VAT paid on mobile phones and mobile phone credit.

Mixed used items are items that serve both for the purpose of the business as well as the personal use, since you cannot precisely ascertain the business use percentage.

No question asked, if the tax office audits your books and finds out you did not reduce the deductible proportion of VAT, you'll need to payback VAT on top of a minimum 120% fine. Not the best deal.

1.2.13. INCOME TAX DEDUCTIBILITY

Regarding income tax the non-deductible part of costs suffered is:
- 100% of any item which is not inherent to your business;
- 80% of vehicle related expenses;
- 50% of mixed used times;
- 20% of mobile phone costs.

Once you have that clear in your mind, you can plan better; but remember that your friend's accountant deducts everything and never got caught!

Please ask your friend if he checked the books properly as you cannot go around this law.

1.2.14. INHERITANCE TAX, DONATION TAX, AND WILL

Every western country has inheritance and donation taxes, which triggers once you transfer part of your wealth to third parties, whether you are alive or at death.

I already know what you are thinking!

You get taxed once you make income; you get taxed once you spend income; you get taxed on wealth and properties while alive, and you get taxed again once you die!

Sad, but true.

Italy, unlike other countries (most notably France and the UK), does not have high inheritance and donation taxes, and they do not account much into the Italian tax budget; however, you must be aware of their existence.

First and foremost, it is extremely important to understand inheritance and donation law; Italy is a Roman law system, and unlike common law countries it has strict rules when it comes to inheritance and donations.

Based on the number of descendants, the law establishes how the wealth is divided among the member included within the issue. Remember also that you have a fixed percentage (which varies depending on the number of descendants) of your personal wealth that you can dispose freely.

Just a quick example: if you are married with three kids, your spouse share is 2/3 of your wealth, while each kid gets 1/3 of the remaining part. During life you could have disposed of no more than 25% of your wealth. No questions asked.

For instance, you cannot assent or donate your whole wealth to one of the sons, or to a third party.

The descendant that did not inherit can appeal that will or the donation and request that it is overturned; the judge conforms to the law and requires the descendant to be reinstated within the issue.

Furthermore, if you have assets in multiple countries, I strongly advise you to write a will which is valid in both jurisdictions and nominates an executor; given that writing such will can be complicated and it requires to be written in more than one language, you should think of hiring an experienced lawyer.

According to the Italian law, the succession procedure takes place in the jurisdiction in which the deceased is a resident, and if no executor is appointed the procedure will be dealt by a local notary. If you have assets abroad, those cannot be transferred until the day the succession process is cleared.

Do you understand why writing a will and nominating an executor becomes crucial?

What falls outside of the inheritance tax scope:

- Italian government bonds;
- Life insurances;
- Partnerships and unquoted shareholdings.

You basically pay it on investment portfolio, real estate properties, cash, boats, and airplanes.

In regards to real estate properties, they are valued at the cadastral value, not the market value; thus, reducing the value for inheritance tax purposes.

The inheritance tax brackets are different based on the relationship with the donor, or the deceased, as well as the nil rate bands.

Note that nil rate bands apply per donee, thus if you donate your wealth to four donees, you must then multiply by four the applicable nil rate band.

RELATIONSHIP	TAX RATE	NIL rate BAND
Spouse or Lineal Descendant	4%	€ 1,000,000
Brother or Sister	6%	€ 100,000
Family Member Within 4 Degrees	6%	
Other	8%	

You can donate € 1,000,000.00 per lineal descendant and not pay a single dime in tax. If you have a son and a daughter you can transfer € 1,000,000.00 to each without triggering any liability now or at death.

Bear also in mind, that you are to pay registrar tax and stamp duty if the property transferred requires so; for instance, if you transfer your house you must pay registrar taxes as any other transfer made on properties.

A common way to save inheritance tax money or to donate wealth to a party which would not be included by the law is the use of life insurance policies.

Life insurance policies are basically investment portfolios administered by a bank or financial institution; unlike investment portfolios the life insurance will include a beneficiary in case of death.

During life the subscriber can dispose of the portfolio and change the ultimate beneficiary at his/her own discretion, and should the investment run at end, the subscriber is the one entitled to deal with it.

Should the subscriber die, the beneficiary can cash in the life insurance, and this falls outside of the scope of inheritance taxes as the life insurance per se is not considered as part of the wealth of the deceased.

Bear in mind, that the bank or the financial institution cannot by law get in touch with the ultimate beneficiary; therefore, it is the latter who must ask for its redemption, and if you are unsure if you are the ultimate beneficiary of a life insurance policy, there is a phone line that can help you out.

The maximum time frame to redeem your life insurance is 10 years, and after that the bank will keep the proceeds.

Given the inflexibility of the Italian inheritance law system, life insurances have proven as an efficient tool for planning; moreover, they have a slightly more advantageous tax treatment of capital gains and dividends with lower administration fees.

1.3. SOCIAL BENEFITS

1.3.1. THE NATIONAL HEALTH SYSTEM

The right to healthcare is one of the basic human rights, without any race, religion, political beliefs, economic, or social condition.

The Italian national healthcare system (SSN) is a universal public service that guarantees healthcare to all its citizens and residents. The SSN is financed through the general taxation system (taxes); however, certain healthcare services require a fee payment (i.e., medical prescriptions, specialist doctor appointments etc.).

Fees are normally waived (or greatly reduced) to low-income households. The main goal of the Italian SSN is not to discriminate its access upon the economic condition.

To register to the Italian SSN. you must register as a resident at the local Comune, then you must enroll at the local ASL obtaining your registration and health card called Tessera Sanitaria or TS.

With your Tessera Sanitaria, you can access the healthcare system and specifically the following services:
- General Practitioner and pediatrician;
- Free hospitalization in public hospitals or private affiliated ones;
- Drugs and prescriptions;
- General medical exams and surgeries;
- Vaccinations;
- Blood tests;
- Rehab and physical assistance.
-

The Italian healthcare system does not exclude from its coverage those individuals who are non-compliant with the immigration regulations. Those individuals can access the basic services provided by the system.

They have access to any urgent or anyway essential hospital and surgery treatments, even continuative, for diseases and accidents. Besides, they are allowed access to preventive medicine programs safeguarding individual and collective health such as vaccinations and infectious diseases treatments.

1.3.2. INPS AND SOCIAL BENEFITS

NPS is the Italian National Insurance Contribution, administering the pension system of Italy.

Normally, you can be enrolled in just one INPS contribution system, and should you do two activities, only the prevailing one must be accounted for INPS contribution purposes. Let's say that you are employed, and you run a side business selling online flipped stuff. You already pay INPS at your employment and you should register at the Gestione Commercianti too. However, your employment prevails, and you are not required to register nor to pay any other contribution.

How many years do you need to contribute to get a pension in the future? To secure a future pension treatment, you are required to contribute into the system for at least 9 full years. If you contribute any less, you will not have the right to receive a pension from the Italian government.

You can opt out to pay INPS if you are a full-time employee (since you already pay it in your payslip). US citizens are also exempted from contributing into the Italian INPS.

INPS payments are tax deductible items against your income, and it is the only allowable item to claim in the forfettario regime. This means that any payment made to INPS will reduce your taxable income, thus creating a tax saving.

INPS also provides Social Benefits to workers and retired people. Most notably INPS provides for unemployment benefits, Babysitter bonus, children bonus, maternity allowance, and lower income support and integration.

1.4. CONCLUSION ON TAXES

As you might have understood, taxes in Italy are fairly complicated and the best strategy you can adopt is to carefully plan your activity and structure it in a tax efficient way.

To do so, you should hire an experienced accountant that ideally speaks your language to guide you through. Once again, never focus on the tax bracket per se, always focus.

2
MOVE YOUR
RESIDENCY CHECKLIST

If you are considering moving to Italy, here is my checklist to avoid any headaches and make the process as smooth as possible:
- Get your Codice Fiscale;
- Find out if you need a VISA;
- If you need a VISA, investigate on restrictions and limitations;
- Audit your income structure;
- Audit your financial income and realize potential capital gains;
- Understand the impact of withholding taxes once you move to Italy;
- Screen your foreign companies against the Esterovestizione risk;
- Look for jobs before moving to Italy;
- Talk to an accountant in regards your tax liabilities.

Once you move to Italy:
- Get a bank account (you can also opt for a nonresident one)
- Rent before buying;
- Get a legal lease contract;
- File your taxes on time.

The most important part of your residency checklist is WHEN you decide to move to Italy! Picking the right time of the year can have enormous consequences on your tax position, as you might become a tax resident of Italy.

2.1. TAX CALENDAR

The Italian tax year is the same as the calendar year, starting from January 1st and ending on December 31st; income is generally taxed on the cash basis; therefore, only income paid during that time frame is taxable in that year. Business income is the most common exception as it is taxed on the accrual basis. In Italy, unlike other countries, you pay taxes BEFORE filing it. Yes, you read it right, in Italy you pay first and then you file your taxes.

The tax return deadline falls on November 30th of the following year; however, there is further 90 days extension for late filings carrying a penalty of € 25.00. Once these 90 days have past, there is no possibility filing a return, and there are no mitigating circumstances to avoid the fines. A return filed after such date will carry a minimum general fine of € 250.00 and up to € 1,000.00 on top of a fine ranging from 120% to 240% of any tax liability resulting from the return itself. Now, do you understand why it is imperative to know if you have to file your taxes or not?

Bear in mind that the tax office has eight years to investigate your personal position and fine you if you did not file your taxes. Unfortunately, many expats realize this too late after the ultimate deadline has passed and they ask to file late returns. At this point the only advice is to keep our fingers crossed and hope the tax office will not audit your position for 8 years (which is becoming increasingly more likely due to the higher informatization of the tax office, as well as the larger cooperation among jurisdictions globally).

The first tax deadline is June 30th, while the second one is November 30th.

There are two tax deadlines as in Italy you pay taxes in ADVANCE; therefore, on June 30th you must pay the balancing payment for the past tax year on top of an advance payment calculated as 40% of the past year tax liability. The remaining 60% falls due on November 30th . Since the payments on account can create a cash outflow issue, it is possible to break the payment due on June 30th into 5 equal instalments falling due at the end of each month up until October 31st.

2.2. GENERAL CONDITIONS TO ENTER ITALY

EU nationals are not required to go through any bureaucracy, while any non-EU national is required to meet ALL the requirements listed below to enter any Schengen area country:
- Enter the EU through a hard border;
- Have a valid Passport (or any equivalent travel document) to enter the EU;
- Have documents substantiating the purpose of the travel;
- Have sufficient means of support, both for the stay period and to return to their country of origin (or to travel to a Third State)
- Have a valid entry VISA (if required);
- Have a clear record in the Schengen Information System (SIS);
- Have a clear criminal record and not be classified as a threat to the national security.

If the non-EU citizen is already a resident of another Schengen State, he is not required to hold a VISA for any stay in Italy of 90 days or less, unless the entry is regarding employment, self-employment, or study reasons.

Bear in mind that you need to meet ALL the above criteria. Failing to meet any of the above elements leads to the denial of entry and the repatriation.

Immigration is ruled primarily at EU level, providing a main legislation framework to which every member State has to comply. Every single Country can provide certain restriction or introduce new VISA types, as long as it is in compliance with the European framework.

2.2.1. WHAT IS A VISA?

A VISA is the authorization given to a non-EU citizen to enter the territory of Italy (or any other Schengen country) for transit or stay.

EFTA citizens (Iceland, Liechtenstein, Norway, San Marino, Switzerland, and Vatican) have the same right of movements as any EU citizen.

A VISA is always required for stay periods exceeding 90 days, whereas, for stays of 90 days or less there are some exceptions for tourism, missions, business, invitations, and sport competitions.

Citizens of the following countries: Andorra, Argentina, Australia, Bolivia, Brazil, Brunei, Canada, Chile, Cyprus, Costa Rica, Ecuador, El Salvador, Guatemala, Honduras, Israel, Japan, Malaysia, Mexico, Nicaragua, New Zealand, Panama, Paraguay, Singapore, South Korea, the United States, Uruguay, and Venezuela do not need any VISA for stays up to 90 days.

VISAs are issued by the foreign Italian consulates around the world, and you need to obtain the VISA prior to attempting to enter Italy. We can briefly sum up that you will need a VISA to stay in Italy 90 days or longer, or if your country does not have a VISA waiver for shorter stays.

You are normally required to apply to the Italian consulate in your jurisdiction of residence. However, if you apply to VISAs for stays up to 90 days, you can apply in any Italian consulate overseas, regardless of its location.

A particular VISA category is available to those individuals who hold a long-term permit of stay, but it has been lost, stolen, or it has expired while staying overseas. Those individuals can apply for a RE-ENTRY VISA.

Visa types
The Italian immigration system provides for multiple VISA available to foreign citizens wishing to enter and settle in Italy. If your

question is "How do I get a VISA to Italy?" you must be aware that there are several options available to you.

The most common VISA is the tourist VISA. If you want to visit Italy and all its beautiful sceneries, cities, and landscape, you must apply for a tourist VISA.

This allows you to stay in Italy for up to 90 non-consecutive days within 180 days; you can roughly approximate it as 3 months on and 3 months off Italy.

If you want to stay longer in Italy, you are required to obtain a long-term VISA, thus you must provide certain criteria to qualify. The main VISA options are:

- Elective Residency;
- Self-employment;
- Corporate position;
- Business;
- Study;
- Research;
- EU Blue Card;
- Employment;
- Investor;
- Family reunification.

There is a wide spectrum of possibilities to obtain a VISA; knowing them will help you strategize better your move to Italy.

2.2.2. PERMESSO DI SOGGIORNO APPLICATION

Permesso di Soggiorno can roughly be translated into Residence Permit. This document authorizes non-EU citizens to regularly reside in Italy and that, as a rule, implies the legal entry in the territory.

You need a VISA to enter Italy and then apply for a Permesso di Soggiorno. The Permesso di Soggiorno allows you to reside in Italy long term. This is a very important concept to grasp; too many people are confused by the two terms.

Permesso di Soggiorno is issued for the following reasons:
- Tourism
- Visits
- Business
- Study or training
- Seasonal work
- Independent and self-employed work
- Employment work,
- Family reasons
- Social protection
- Medical treatments
- International protection seekers and international protection.

To apply for a Permesso di Soggiorno, you must fill your application within 8 working days from your entry in the Italian territory. The clock starts from the date on which the border police put the entry stamp on your passport. The application is normally submitted to any Post office accredited with the Sportello Amico; there are few exceptions to that rule for certain specific applications.

If you are applying for business, medical treatments, humanitarian reasons, international protection application, minors, justice, granting of the status of stateless person, or minor's integration permits, you must submit your application to the Immigration office of the Questura located in the province in which you have your domicile.

You must apply to the Single Desk at the immigration office if you are applying for subordinate/employment work or family re-unification permit.

In most of the application, you must apply to the local post office. While writing, I imagine you comfortably sitting on your sofa rolling your eyes because you are well-aware of the long queue you are about to face to simply submit your application.

The good news is that the post office has a mobile application allowing you to book an appointment beforehand, thereby skipping the whole queue. I cannot stress enough the importance of booking your slot in advance unless you enjoy waiting in line for hours.

To submit your application, you must provide the following documents:

1. Valid passport or other equivalent document showing the applicant's nationality, date, and place of birth;
2. Codice Fiscale;
3. Entry VISA;
4. Documents proving your current domicile (residence certificate or hospitality statement);
5. Document proving the availability of the necessary means of support to return to the country of provenance, except for residence permits for family and work reasons;
6. 4 passport-size photographs;
7. Documents relating to the specific residence permit (e.g., employment contract, Partita IVA certificate, investment certificates etc.).

Documents 1-2-3 are not required for social and international protection or if the individual applies for the Italian citizenship as a stateless person.

Applications are subject to a contribution ranging from € 40 to € 100 depending on the type of residence permit, payable in cash or via debit/credit card at the post office.

International protection seekers, international protection and humanitarian protection applications are free of charge.

Once the application is done and the post office clerk has made sure of your ID and verified that all the documents are submitted, you will receive an appointment date to the local immigration office to provide your fingerprints. This completes the application process.

Meanwhile, you will receive a paper receipt which includes all your personal information application, and it serves for the purpose of the Permesso itself until you complete the process at the immigration office.

2.2.3. EU RESIDENCE PERMIT

Residence Permits are normally available exclusively in the country of application. However, the EU introduced an EU residence Permit where the applicant is provided the freedom to move and work in all EU Member States.

EU residence permit application
To be granted an EU long term residence permit, the applicant must meet the following requirements:
- 5 years of residence in Italy;
- Annual Income exceeding the social allowance threshold;
- Italian language proficiency test (A2 level).

Certain individuals cannot apply for the EU long term residence permit, such as:
- Study permit holders;
- Temporary protection/humanitarian permit holders;
- International protection seekers;
- Voluntary work, diplomatic reasons or special missions permit holders;
- VISA holders or short-term residence permit holders;
- Any foreign citizen considered as a threat to the National security.

The 5 years clock also includes any period during which the applicant fell under any of the above categories.

You can only apply at a suitable Post office, providing the following documents:

1. Valid passport;
2. Current residence permit;
3. Codice Fiscale;
4. Courthouse criminal charges clearing certificate;
5. Documents proving your current domicile (residence certificate or hospitality statement)
6. Proof of income availability;
7. Residence certificate and family status certificate (if the application also involves family members);
8. 4 passport-size photographs

2.2.4. RIGHTS PROVIDED

EU long term residence permit holders are allowed to:
- Enter Italy without any visa and move freely in the EU;
- Carry employment, self-employment work, notwithstanding any work legally reserved to citizens or prohibited to foreigners;
- Access welfare, national insurance protections, as well as healthcare, educational, and social services;
- Vote for the municipality mayor.

The EU residence permit is a milestone to be achieved and it is the penultimate step prior to acquiring the Italian citizenship, then you can say goodbye to any EU immigration office ever.

Holding this type of Residence Permit grants almost the same rights as Italian citizens.

However, there are certain conditions under which the EU residence permit is revoked if:
- Acquired by fraud;
- The holder is deported;

- The holder becomes a threat to the National security;
- The applicant is absent from the EU for 12 consecutive months;
- The applicant is absent from Italy for 6 years;
- The permit is issued by another Member State of the European Union;
- The status of refugee or of subsidiary protection is terminated or revoked.

2.3. HOW TO PAY TAXES IN ITALY

Let's get practical now! How do you pay taxes in Italy? At this point I am sure you understand how to calculate your taxes, tax deductions, foreign tax credits etc. However, how do you transfer money from you to the tax office? I have to admit that Italy has come a long way to simplify the way to pay taxes as the digitalization of the payments has been a reality for decades.

F24 (pronounced "effe24") is the main tax form used to pay almost every tax. The great thing about this form is that you can offset tax credits and tax debits, as well as identify every single tax you pay with a different tax code given by the office. It is then very easy to track down the payments you made.

But how do you practically pay this form? You have multiple options to do it. The first one is to pay at the local post office or at every bank in cash (up to € 3,000.00): you show up with three copies of the form, pay the bottom amount, and retain a copy as a proof of payment. There is no charge for such service.

The second option is to pay through your home banking; almost every Italian bank has developed a portal from which you can pay the form online; you type in the taxes due and the payable amounts, and the game is done. The third option is to do everything on the Agenzia delle Entrate website. In this case, you must include the IBAN of your Italian bank account from which you want taxes to be paid.

If you have troubles in dealing with the F24 forms, you can provide your tax accountant with your IBAN and he/she will take care of the payment. In this case, the accountant does not have access to your funds as he/she simply instructs the tax office to withdraw that money, on a given day, with the scope of paying taxes.

Unlike the other solutions mentioned before, the accountant might charge a fee for this service.

Often, I prefer this solution for my clients as I can keep track of their payments and make sure they always fit within the deadline without incurring late payment fines or penalties.

In every case you must use a bank account with your Codice Fiscale, and you cannot pay taxes from another person's bank account as the control system will reject the whole payment.

All the aforementioned solutions require you to either be in Italy physically or to have an Italian bank account; so how do you pay taxes if you are not in Italy, and you do not have an Italian bank account? This is a common scenario for people who bought a second home in Italy and do not live here; often they do not have a local bank account and the only tax they must pay in Italy is the Property Tax (IMU). In such case, you must do an international bank wire to the tax office. I strongly discourage doing it as, unlike the F24 payments, there is no digital track of it, and the tax office finds it difficult to match the payment to the liability which often results in auditing letters to be issued. As long as you have the proof of payment, there is no problem to challenge the audit letter; however, this increases the paperwork to be dealt with, and I do not recommend it.

Finally, always bear in mind that your accountant CANNOT pay taxes on your behalf! It used to be a common practice to transfer the money on your accountant's bank account and he/she will pay taxes from it.

NEVER DO THAT!

There have been hundreds of horrific stories about this scheme where the accountant received the monies from the clients, embezzling the funds without paying any single dime in taxes. Honestly, I am still surprised that people keep doing it.

The main problem here is that you need to sue your accountant, start a trial, pay a lawyer, and after some years you might get some money back. In the meantime, the tax office will request the payments to be performed on top of a late payment fine. In the end, you pay your taxes twice and you need to sue your accountant to get the money back. Not the best thing to happen.

2.4. CODICE FISCALE

The Codice Fiscale is the Italian unique code to identify every individual (and companies too). This concept exists in many jurisdictions: in the US they call it Social Security Number, and in the UK, it is called National Insurance Number.

If you are born in Italy, you are assigned your Codice Fiscale at birth; in every other case you must request one.

The Codice Fiscale serves multiple purposes, and without it you are refrained to perform many simple daily tasks, such as:
- Setting up a bank account;
- Sign a rent lease;
- Sign an employment contract;
- Get a Partita IVA;
- Request your Universal Health Care coverage;
- Enroll in school;
- Request residency in Italy.

As you can tell, getting a Codice Fiscale is a cornerstone of your life in Italy. Without it, you cannot really do anything. How do you get a Codice Fiscale and where do you apply for it?

Requesting a Codice Fiscale is a simple process as you need to fill a paper form with your personal information (full name, date and place of birth, citizenship, and a domicile), and attach a valid ID.

In my experience, I always advise to provide a foreign address to avoid any confusion regarding your tax position in Italy. Filling the form with an Italian address might, in very rare cases, be used as a declaration of residency of tax purposes. You can win against that in court, but you still need to start a trial and win it.

You can get your Codice Fiscale personally or you can delegate someone to do it on your behalf. Every Italian tax office as well as any consulate or embassy around the world can issue that instantly.

Having a Codice Fiscale has nothing to do with tax residency. Everybody can request a Codice Fiscale and never visit or pay tax to Italy. It is just an identification code, nothing more and nothing less.

If you plan to move to Italy, my keenest advice is to get the Codice Fiscale ahead of time. This allows you to save a lot of time and start ahead to get personal and tax matters sorted swiftly.

2.5. REGISTER AT THE TOWN HALL

Once you enter Italy with your VISA, you are finally ready to settle and register at the local town hall to benefit of the same treatment as any other citizen or resident of Italy.

To do so, you are required to file an application to the local Municipality. Unfortunately, there is not a single online portal to do it, and you must check with your local municipality on the required process. Milan council allows the residency application to be filed online through their portal, while other municipalities require the whole process to be filed in a very old-fashioned way.

In any case, you must submit your passport, along your residency permit, your codice fiscale, and your lodging information (declaration of hospitality, house ownership, or rental agreement). You must also submit the relevant papers to your employment or self-employment. If you lack of this, you must show proof of at least € 6,000 in a bank account to support your application.

If you are in Italy under an Elective Residence VISA, you are also required to provide a valid private annual health insurance to back your registration.

Non-resident bank account.

If you have made the decision to buy a house in Italy, you are very likely to pay a down payment upfront while signing the deed. The amount of the required down payment varies depending on the area in which you decide to buy property, as well as the type of the property you buy. This payment is very easy to execute as you can set up a bank wire from your foreign bank account to the seller's bank account. At this point, the last step is to sign the deed in front of the notary, which I again remind you can be executed by another person whom you give power of attorney.

Sometimes, real estate agents fail to disclose that you are required to pay the balancing payment and the taxes due, and that the only way to make that payment is by using an old-school payment document that is required by Italian Law, the assegno circolare. The assegno circolare is not a bank check, the issuing bank guarantees the funds to be available, thus reducing the chances of a bounce back to 0%. But why would the notary only accept this old-fashioned payment method? It is a means of reducing risk. The assegno circolare verifies that the money is guaranteed by the bank, so the Notary can be 100% sure he/she is not a victim of a fraudulent scheme.

Now comes the tricky part! The notary only accepts the assegno circolare. To obtain an assegno circolare, you need to have a local bank account. If you walk into the local bank, especially in smaller cities, the local clerk cannot process your request if you are not a resident of Italy, and they only work with local bank accounts.

If you try to ask your foreign bank, it will not help you through the process. Even if you can get such a check from a non-Italian bank, the Italian notary will likely turn it down as the bank is not Italian. It sounds like you might reach a dead end at this point, and you cannot get the house you already put a down payment on, nor can you get the down payment back. This can be a nightmare scenario for a non-Italian resident, and one that may spoil your dream of becoming an Italian homeowner! Thankfully there is a solution.

The solution is a non-resident bank account. The non-resident bank account is, as the word says, a bank account for individuals who do not have a residency in Italy, and it is run by a local authorized bank, thus solving any potential denials of you right to the property.

All you need to setup a non-resident bank account is:
– Codice Fiscale (which you also need to buy a property)
– Valid ID
– Proof of residency abroad

With this information and a bunch of signatures, you will then have an Italian based bank account that works the same as a resident bank account.

Now all you must do is transfer funds from your foreign bank account to the Italian one, and when you are ready to sign the deed, you need to ask you bank for the assegno circolare. Even though the non-resident bank account is more expensive than the local ones (from € 5.00 to € 20.00 in monthly fees), this is the fastest and safest way to handle a property purchase in 22 Italy if you are a non-resident; finally, once you become a resident in Italy, you can turn your bank account into a local one, saving on the monthly fees. If you decide not to become a resident of Italy you can keep the non-resident account, so you can domicile you bills, utilities, and your property tax payments while you are abroad.

3

WHAT TO DO
AND NOT DO

3.1. HOW DOES THE BIG BROTHER KNOWS WHAT I AM DOING?

> *"Know your enemy and know yourself and you can fight a hundred battles without disaster."*
> Sun Tzu

I could not find a better quote to introduce this chapter. Despite Sun Tzu is referring to war scenarios, knowing your enemy and knowing yourself is the only way to succeed in every human activity including mastering your taxes in Italy. You must know how the tax office gets the right information and knocks at your door asking for your share.

The first big source of data is data provided by every taxpayer, such as:

- Tax returns;
- Tax payments;
- Lease contracts;
- Codice Fiscale;
- Partita IVA;
- Every single invoice since 2019!

This is clear, as you are required to file returns and pay taxes to the tax office, that they can definitely use that information to run any type of control they want. Furthermore, since the early 2000's the Italian tax office has developed enormously towards the informatization and digitalization of its structure. Every information has to be filed electronically, and the tax office then has an xml file available; you should stop thinking of the tax office as a pile of old papers and desks filled with handwritten tax returns. You should think of them as a huge library of personal information of every taxpayer which can be enquired in few seconds.

On top of that, the tax office has unlimited access without any permission request to data available in other public offices databases:
- Residency details;
- Bank details;
- Public notary information;
- Department of motor vehicles information;
- Chamber of Commerce registration.

Essentially, the tax office can access every information available in every public office without your consent.

Currently, the tax office has an unbelievable amount of data available, and it structures its controls on two main levels:
1. Automatic controls;
2. Paper based controls;

Automatic controls
This is the most basic and automated control performed by the tax office; it consists of cross-checking data available in different databases in their possession. A common example is prompt tax payment controls. The tax office cross-checks information available in the tax return and compares it with the flow of payments available; they can then realize if the taxpayer has paid enough taxes, and if the payments were performed on/before the tax payment deadlines. Should you have paid less than due or later than due, the tax office will send you a letter highlighting the amounts due as well as the applicable fine.

Automatic controls are not overseen by any individual and often they result in inaccurate fines; however, it is very easy to correct them, and if you provide the accurate information, they can easily withdraw the "fine".

This is to show that the system is not always right as the detection software still makes mistakes.

Paper based control

Paper based controls are the next level controls, operated by an inspector. If you think about it, automatic controls are very cheap to run; however, they have a huge limitation as they can only check data available in their systems. Tax returns are made of boxes and several costs/revenues are not segregated; therefore, the tax office only sees a number but not the actual breakdown. The only way to understand how every box is made up is to take a look at the supporting documents. Anyway, since the returns are filed without any attachment, how can they get ahold of that? Simple! They send you a letter with a written request to show papers regarding certain matters. You then need to go to the tax office in person, or delegate someone to do it on your behalf, to provide such information. If the information is accurate, you will have no problems; otherwise, you might get fines and sanctions due to inaccurate returns, as well as a recalculation of your tax liability.

But how do they choose to perform paper-based controls?

Normally, if any box in your tax return results as an outlier compared to similar data, a flag is shown, and a tax inspector might run an investigation on that. The system is looking for anomalies and outlier data to narrow down the investigation with the highest likelihood of being successful.

3.1.1. INFORMATION EXCHANGE

A common strategy for Italian tax dodgers was to incorporate businesses overseas, or to put their money in an offshore account. Too bad that jurisdictions are currently exchanging tax and financial information among them.

The EU is implementing the DAC 6 protocol, which automatically exchange information such as:
- employment income;
- pension income
- Financial accounts values
- Investment accounts values
- Dividends and financial income

OECD countries adopt CRS information exchange, to which you may add FATCA and general information exchange approved by the double tax treaties signed among countries.

Hiding your cash offshore is no longer an option, and the Italian tax office may get that information sooner or later. Your best solution is to plan your finances accordingly and structure your income and your finances in the most efficient way should you become a tax resident of Italy.

3.2. WHY ALWAYS ME?

Have you ever asked yourself why the tax office has decided to audit you instead of somebody else? Do you think it is just misfortune? Not really! There is a motivation that triggers an audit from the tax office, and I will explain it. But first, you must understand how the whole audit system works in Italy. Every year, the Department of Economics and Finance of Italy sets out the directives regarding audits, identifying the business sectors and industries at higher risk of tax evasion and tax dodging.

The directive is based on tax office data as well as National Statistics Institute (ISTAT) data, and it also defines the required goals to tackle the phenomenon of tax evasion. The goals then set out the number of the required audits and the business sectors to audit; these audits are then divided among the different tax offices located throughout Italy.

A common strategy to reduce your risk of being audited is the place of incorporation or residency. Think of the risk of being audited as a lottery; the tax office draws a number, and the misfortune company will be audited. Since number matters, do you think you have the same chance of "winning" if the participants are 10,000 or 100,000? Absolutely no!

The same happens with audits: if you are incorporated in crowded areas where there are more lottery participants, you are less likely to be audited! The tax office knows that and provides more resources and personnel to larger areas; anyway, this is not sufficient, and imbalances exist. It is, therefore, less likely to be audited if you are incorporated in Milan, instead of Bergamo.

This first conclusion has effects on the place of incorporation; this is totally legal, and you have the right to incorporate wherever you want. Have you thought about that? Having said that, you still have a chance to be audited regardless of your incorporation place. Let me explain how the audit works. One morning the tax office knocks at your door. Panic! You are not used to deal with the tax man; moreover, they just showed up without notice. Always open the door and be gentle; any strategy to delay or postpone the investigation is not well welcomed, and more importantly it does not help you.

Every audit needs to be motivated! The auditor will show a paper outlining the scope of the audit and the motivation that lead to the inspection; you can take your time reading it and you have the right to be assisted by an accountant. The auditors can access to the documents outlined in the letter and cannot extend the investigation to further papers and letters. If they ask you to provide further documents at this stage, you can politely refuse and offer your availability to show them at due course. I also advice to log all the activities the auditors perform as if there is any irregularity you can appeal to the Garante del Contribuente which, among other duties, oversees the auditors works. It is free and you do not need any attorney; you can simply send a letter to them, and they will investigate.

After completing the audit, the inspectors must write a report that you can sign. You have the right to take a look at it, add notes, and receive a copy. The auditor will ask you to sign it, but you are not required to if you do not want to. The most common mistakes are:

- Not reading the report;
- Not adding notes and stating that you will show any missing papers at due course;
- Signing the report if unclear.

The most important mistake is the third one: remember that your signature is extremely important, and the auditors know that; if you sign the report, it means that you agree with EVERYTHING written therein. In other words, you cannot challenge the report later if you signed it. The auditors have many rights, but they also have various obligations, as they cannot do whatever they want!

For instance, the auditors cannot remove the accounting books from the office (yet they can take copies); they cannot access private homes and accounting firm offices without a warrant (unless you open the door and let them in). These are your rights and there is nothing wrong in doing so; however, you must be aware of what you can and cannot do; if you are in doubt, call your accountant!

The auditors cannot have access, unless they gather enough evidence, to personal lockers, bags, purses, and wallets as long as you don't show them. They have the right to ask, and you have the right to refuse. If you decide to cooperate, you must be aware that is YOUR choice, and you will bear the consequences of it.

Once the audit is over, you can always appeal it at court and start a tax litigation.

3.3. WHAT HAPPENS IF YOU DO NOT PAY TAXES?

There are multiple reasons behind it: you might have forgotten, or you did not have access to the online platform to actually pay it, or you simply did not have enough money to pay, or you purely do not want to pay taxes. The intention here does not matter at all; what is important is the fact that you were required to pay, and you did not. What can you do?

3.3.1. RAVVEDIMENTO OPEROSO

If you did not pay on time, and you did not receive a letter from the tax office or you are in the midst of a tax investigation, you can pay yourself through the ravvedimento operoso.

This is a system to calculate the late payment fine, and it is proportionate to the delay; the longer it takes you to pay, the more you pay.

Let's assume that you missed a payment deadline, and the amount owed was € 1,000.00; the chart sums up the fines applicable:

DELAY	FINE Applicable	FINE Payable
1 to 14 days	0.1% per day	€ 1.00 to € 14.00
from 15 to 30 days	1.5%	€ 15.00
from 30 to 90 days	3.75%	€ 37.50
within 1 year	4.29%	€ 42.90
within 2 years	5%	€ 50.00

Should the tax office find out that you did not pay your taxes on time, and you did not perform the ravvedimento operoso, the applicable fines are much higher.

The tax office can issue two types of letters:

1. Invito alla compliance;
2. Avviso di irregolarità.

Both letters do not refer to any audit carried out by the tax office, and they provide the chance to the taxpayer to pay what is due with a reduced fine before the ordinary fine kicks in.

If you receive a Invito alla Compliance, you must pay a fine of 15%, whereas if you receive an avviso di irregolarità, you can pay within 30 days with a fine ranging from 10% to 20% of the ordinary fine (usually 90% of the tax liability); your fine will then be either 9% or 18% of the extra tax to be paid.

Once you receive those letters, the next step is the audit; therefore, it is always advisable to pay, and if you cannot pay in full you can still opt to pay in instalments.

If the total due is less than € 5,000.00, you can request up to 8 quarterly instalments; if the total due is more than that, you can request up to 20 quarterly instalments.

If you don't have any money available, it does not matter how many instalments you can break the payment down as well as the applicable fine. If your ability to pay is 0, you won't make any payment, in any circumstance. Period.

Now that the Agenzia delle Entrate has already done its things and you did not pay your dues, it is time to introduce you Agenzia delle Entrate little brother named Agenzia delle Entrate Riscossione.

Agenzia delle Entrate Riscossione will issue a cartella which is an ultimate request to pay your dues.

At this point you can either pay in 60 monthly instalments or in a single payment.

Once again, what happens if you do not pay?

Agenzia delle Entrate Riscossione has the power to freeze your bank accounts, put your assets on sale (including your residential properties), as well as withhold up to 20% of your salary until you will pay your debt.

If you have any unpaid tax you are also prevented to participate in many public tenders, you cannot ask for tax refunds, and you can seriously harm your personal wealth as well as your business stability.

Reaching the point of having to deal with the Agenzia delle Entrate Riscossione is not good, and it will likely ignite a downward spiral that will not end well.

Once you have to pay taxes, the best strategy is to comply 100% and to try to make the payment before the Agenzia delle Entrate Riscossione is activated; however, if you find yourself always in cash crunches due to impossibility of paying taxes, the answer might lie elsewhere.

You most likely need to sit down with an experienced accountant and restructure the way in which you carry your business; planning your tax expenditure is the best way to save on it!

3.4. BEING RIGHT COSTS. A LOT!

Yes, you read it right! Being right costs time and money.

This is by far the most important lesson I learned from my experience as a tax litigator, representing clients in court against the tax office.

Especially if you run a business, taxes must be treated as a cost, and you must always study every tax decision based on the possible alternative options considering the risks associated with that choice (including the chance of a tax litigation) and the money saving.

You must then always have in your mind these two variables: time and money.

Let me explain how the whole tax litigation system works.

If you receive a letter from the tax office (i.e., you owe them taxes or fines, or they deny you a tax refund), you have 60 days from the day you received the letter to appeal that letter and sue the tax office.

If you fail to sue within the 60 days, you lose the right to appeal and you must abide to the tax office claim, whether it is right or wrong! No mitigating factors apply.

If you think about other judicial matters, unlike tax litigation, you normally have several months or even years to sue the counterpart; 60 days is a very narrow timeframe to build a great and effective strategy. Time does not play in favor of the taxpayer in tax litigation cases.

Before that, if there is any mistake, you can go to the office correct it. Assume that you filled a tax form improperly or the tax office digital infrastructure does not match data available to them; you show the required supporting evidence to the office, and they can amend the letter or withdraw it.

This process is called Autotutela, and for some matters it can also be done online.

Bear in mind that the autotutela does not stop the 60 days clock.

If you still have the pending letter, you are left with no other choice than to appeal it.

Based on the amount challenged, you are required to start through the ADR and negotiate an agreement with the tax office, otherwise you can go straight to court.

Tax litigation cases also require paying to go to court. In fact, on top of court fee (which varies depending on the value challenged and cannot exceed € 1,500.00) you must pay 1/3 of the amount challenged before starting the trial.

Assuming you received a letter that requires you to pay € 9,000.00; you must pay € 120.00 in court fees and € 3,000.00 to start the process. Crazy!

Remember also that you cannot represent yourself if the challenged amount exceeds € 5,000.00; you then need to appoint either a tax accountant or a lawyer.

Once you have done that, the trial finally starts, and the time frame is relatively short given that you normally have a judgement within 1 year.

Normally, the unsuccessful party has to pay the other party's legal fees.

- Before starting a trial, you must consider:
- The tax payments to be made;
- Your attorney's fees;
- The risk associated with the trial;
- The time required to obtain a judgement;
- In case of unsuccessful claim, you must also pay the other party legal fees.

As I stated before, you must always consider if the legal action is convenient on the finance side.

The unsuccessful party can appeal the judgement to the upper tax tribunal, and it can only appeal against the unsuccessful claims; furthermore, you cannot provide any additional evidence as of the first trial.

You can still appeal the judgement on points of matters and points of law.

The bad news is that you have 60 days to appeal the previous judgement, and you must pay the remaining 2/3 of the claim.

Basically, you end up paying all the dues.

Once again, the unsuccessful party can appeal the judgement to the highest court of Italy: the Corte di Cassazione. At this third level you can only challenge the matters of law and you must appoint a lawyer since tax accountant cannot represent at the Corte di Cassazione. Once the judgement is final, there is no further appeal, and the decision is "finally" binding between the parties involved.

Note that at every level the trial can be sent back to the first or second tribunal to restart, thus the timing involved can be incredibly long.

Just to mention one of the longest cases in tax litigation, many Italian artists challenged a decision made by the tax office in 1997 which was finally settled in 2016. 19 YEARS!!!

Once you have the whole process clear in your mind, you can easily understand the statement made at the beginning. Being right costs. A lot!

Is there a way to save money on taxes and avoid a lengthy and consuming trial?

Yes, there is. Actually, there are two other procedures to avoid the trial:

- Acquiescenza;
- Accertamento con adesione.

My first tax supervisor had a very important line about the tax office. "You can always negotiate with them [tax office]! Once you negotiated the amount, you start negotiating the terms of payment."

He was/is more than right!

Acquiescenza is a sort of plea. You waive your right to appeal the decision and in turn you pay 1/3 of the fines due.

Essentially, you pay taxes in full, but the fine is reduced; on top of it, you can pay it in installments.

Accertamento con adesione is a negotiation in which the taxpayer settles both the tax due and the fines. The taxpayer starts a negotiation with the tax office proposing a settlement agreement; the tax office can deny or accept it.

If the accertamento is denied, then you need to start a tax litigation; if accepted, you definitely saved on taxes and time!

The Accertamento con adesione is often used as a way to earn more time before appealing, as it stops the 60 days clock.

Now, do you understand why you need to invest in a consultant that knows what to do?

Planning always beats improvising. Every time!

If you want to settle your base in Italy frame the QRcode below and book an appointment to get guided by my studio.

Made in United States
Troutdale, OR
10/25/2024

24115102R00042